PARTY FOOD
FOR KIDS

Consultant Editor:
Valerie Ferguson

southwater

Contents

Introduction

What could be more exciting and magical for kids than a party – made extra-special by stunning, colourful and scrumptious food? This book is brimming with ideas for all aspects of the menu, both savoury and sweet, including drinks. There are snappy sandwiches and light bites; mouth-watering desserts, cookies and bakes; and wonderful fruity drinks and nibbles. Kids are bound to adore the Sandwich Train and Pizza Faces, as well as the Strawberry Smoothie & Stars-in-your-eyes Biscuits.

Pride of place, however, naturally goes to the cake. Recipes are given for the basic sponge and various types of icing, followed by detailed instructions for six designs, from Teddy's Birthday to Computer Game, suitable for kids of different ages. You can copy the ideas or use them as a starting point to let your imagination soar. Be creative!

The kids will be counting the days to the party, and some of that excitement can go into helping you prepare: many of the recipes can be made by the children themselves.

Kids' parties are always hard work for their parents, but they can also be hugely enjoyable and rewarding. Let this book help you make your kid's party a day to remember.

Planning the Party

When throwing a kids' party, you cannot be too well organized. Careful forward planning will make everything go with a swing.

Choosing a Day & Time

First decide on the date, which may be determined by an event such as a birthday, though the nearest weekend may be more convenient. During the summer, you may find that lots of friends are away, so it is worth checking with the most important guests before you choose a day. Late afternoon parties are more traditional, but for young children lunchtime may be a better bet, when they are at their liveliest. Do not make the party too long.

Venue

If possible, use one room for games and another for the party meal, so that you can prepare the table while the partygoers are busy elsewhere and afterwards close the door on the mess until everyone has gone. Clear as much floor space as you can for games and be sure to stow away precious ornaments and sharp objects.

Numbers

Kids will have firm ideas about who they want at their party. A lot depends on the sort of party you are having, the age of the children and the space available, but try to make sure that the numbers do not get out of hand.

Theme

A fancy dress theme is one way to get the whole party off to a good start. Try to avoid anything too complicated which involves hours of work for parents. A few examples are: pirates, circus theme, zoo party, nursery rhymes, monster party and Vikings.

Entertainment

Many parents opt to engage a professional children's entertainer for the afternoon, particularly for the four to eight age group. The entertainment usually consists of magic tricks, clowning and storytelling – audience participation is welcome! The show is usually about an hour long, finishing just in time for refreshments.

Older children (nine to twelve) enjoy parties based around an activity such as skating, swimming or football.

Invitations

Send out invitations in good time. Either buy invitation cards or let the children make them. If your party is going to have a theme, it is nice to design invitations that go with it. Include all the necessary details and say if it is a fancy dress party, or if you want your guests to bring their swimming things, for instance.

Lists

Keep a list of everyone you send invitations to, and check them off as they reply. With your child, make a list of the sort of food you are going to serve and make another list of games you could play. Then you can make your shopping list: apart from food, drinks and cake ingredients, you will need to remember decorations, balloons and prizes.

Kids' Party Checklist
- Send invitations
- Organize professional children's entertainer, if using
- Book activity, if using
- Plan party menu: snack bags or range of children's party foods and soft drinks
- Order ice, if needed
- Buy decorations and paper tableware
- Buy prizes and party gift bags
- Buy food and drink
- Choose party games and prepare props

Shopping

Large supermarkets sell nearly everything you will need for your party. Look in your local toy shop for novelties that can be used for decorating cakes, as well as for prizes and small presents.

Decorations

Paper chains, streamers and balloons will help to set the party atmosphere. This is definitely an aspect of the preparation that the kids will want to help with.

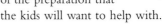

The Party Table

Use paper plates and cups so nothing gets broken. You could also buy a plain white paper cloth and get the kids to decorate it.

Games, Prizes & Presents

If you are planning some competitive games, you will need a stash of tiny prizes to give to the winners. And do not forget to get ready any props you will need for party games (a thimble, a blindfold, a multi-layered parcel and so on). Buy a selection of small gifts to fill the inevitable party bags to give to the kids when they leave.

Sandwich Train

This is a simple way to make sandwiches more appealing to small children, who can sometimes be difficult to please.

Makes 2 trains

INGREDIENTS
2 wholemeal sandwich rounds made with
    soft filling
1 cucumber
radishes
a little sandwich filling
1 celery stick
1 carrot
1 cooked beetroot
cream cheese, lettuce and pretzel stick,
    to garnish (optional)

1 Remove the crusts from the sandwiches and then cut each one into four squares. Cut each of the squares in half again to make eight small sandwiches in total.

2 Make an engine using three of the prepared sandwiches. Arrange the remaining sandwiches behind the engine, placing strips of cucumber skin between them to resemble the railway tracks, reserving a piece.

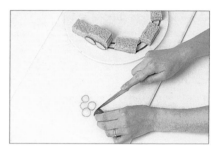

3 Slice the radishes, reserving a piece, and stick on to the sides of the train with a little sandwich filling.

4 Dice the celery, carrot, reserving a piece, and beetroot and pile on to the trucks to resemble the train's cargo.

VARIATIONS: You do not have to stick to these ingredients for decorating the train. Other colourful vegetables could be used instead: chopped red, green and yellow peppers would work well, as would sweetcorn. Make extra greenery from watercress if you like.

5 Cut a carrot funnel, top with cream cheese smoke if liked and place on the engine with half a radish, and a piece of cucumber. If you want to make a tree, tie some lettuce on to a pretzel stick and stick it in position with a blob of cream cheese.

Log Cabin

This eye-catching construction takes a little time to make, but is a great favourite with children.

Makes 1 cabin (18 sandwiches)

INGREDIENTS
4 wholemeal sandwich rounds
    made with chosen filling,
    crusts removed
pretzel sticks
50 g/2 oz/¼ cup curd cheese
1 tomato
1 carrot
1 radish
2.5 cm/1 in piece cucumber

1 Place two of the prepared sandwich rounds on a board and cut each one into six small, rectangular sandwiches. Then cut each of the two remaining sandwich rounds into four equal triangular shapes.

2 Stack the rectangular sandwiches together to form the base of the cabin and place six of the triangle shapes on top to form the roof. (You can serve the rest of the sandwich triangles separately.)

3 Arrange the pretzel sticks on the roof to look like logs, sticking them on with a little sandwich filling or curd cheese if necessary.

4 Break the remaining pretzel sticks into 2.5 cm/1 in lengths and use to make a fence around the cabin, sticking in position with curd cheese.

5 Cut the tomato into doors and windows. Cut the carrot into a chimney, attach it using curd cheese and add some curd cheese smoke. Cut flowers from radishes and carrots. Dice the cucumber finely and arrange to resemble a path.

Sailing Boats

A novelty sandwich that you can prepare with many different fillings.

Makes 12 boats

INGREDIENTS
6 bridge rolls
225 g/8 oz chosen filling (see Cook's Tip)
chopped fresh parsley
2 tomatoes, quartered and seeded
2 radishes
6 processed cheese slices

1 Cut each roll in half horizontally and trim the base so that it stands evenly. Put 15 ml/1 tbsp of the filling on to each half and spread to the edges, doming it slightly.

2 Surround the filling with a border of chopped parsley if you like. Cut the tomatoes into thin strips and arrange round the edge of each half-roll.

3 Cut the radishes into strips and two triangles. Cut the cheese slices into sail shapes.

4 Thread each of the sails on to a cocktail stick and stand in the filling, supporting it with some radish strips if necessary.

COOK'S TIPS: To make peanut and tomato filling for sandwiches, mix together 45 ml/3 tbsp crunchy peanut butter and 45 ml/3 tbsp tomato chutney.
To make cheese and pineapple filling, thoroughly combine 115 g/4 oz/½ cup curd cheese with 30 ml/2 tbsp drained and chopped canned pineapple and add seasoning to taste.

Chilli Cheese Nachos

Make this snack as spicy as you like by adjusting the amount of chillies.

Serves 4

INGREDIENTS
115 g/4 oz bag chilli tortilla chips
50 g/2 oz/½ cup Cheddar cheese, grated
50 g/2 oz/½ cup Red Leicester cheese, grated
50 g/2 oz pickled green jalapeño chillies,
    sliced, or to taste

FOR THE DIP
30 ml/2 tbsp lemon juice
1 avocado, peeled, stoned and
    roughly chopped
1 beefsteak tomato, roughly chopped
salt and freshly ground pepper

1 Arrange the tortilla chips in an even layer on a flameproof plate. Sprinkle with the grated cheeses and scatter jalapeño chillies to taste over the top.

2 Put the plate under a hot grill and toast until the cheese has melted and browned a little.

3 Mix the lemon juice, avocado and tomato together in a bowl and add salt and pepper to taste. Serve the chilli cheese nachos hot with the avocado and tomato salsa.

Bacon Twists

These savoury home-made bread rolls, in a fun shape, will add an extra twist to a kids' party. Serve with soft, herbed cheese.

Makes 12

INGREDIENTS
450 g/1 lb/4 cups strong
  white flour
6 g/¼ oz sachet easy-blend
  dried yeast
2.5 ml/½ tsp salt
400 ml/14 fl oz/1⅔ cups
  hand-hot water
12 streaky bacon rashers
1 egg, beaten

2 Turn the dough on to a lightly floured surface and then knead for 5 minutes or until it is smooth and stretchy. Divide into 12 pieces and roll each one into a sausage shape.

1 Place the flour, yeast and salt in a bowl and stir together. Add a little of the hand-hot water and mix with a knife. Add the remaining water and use your hands to pull the mixture together, to make a sticky dough.

3 Lay each bacon rasher on a chopping board and run the back of the knife down its length, to stretch it slightly. Wind a rasher of bacon round each dough "sausage".

COOK'S TIP: To test whether the "sausages" are done, tap the base of one gently – if it sounds hollow, it's cooked.

VARIATION: The same basic dough mix can be used to make rolls or a loaf of bread.

4 Brush the "sausages" with beaten egg and arrange them on a lightly oiled baking sheet. Leave somewhere warm for 30 minutes or until they have doubled in size. Preheat the oven to 200°C/400°F/Gas 6 and cook the "sausages" for 20–25 minutes until they are cooked and browned. Serve them warm.

Mini Sausage Rolls

Everyone loves sausage rolls and children are no exception. These miniature versions are just the right size for small mouths.

Makes 40

INGREDIENTS

15 g/½ oz/1 tbsp butter
1 onion, finely chopped
350 g/12 oz good-quality sausage meat
15 ml/1 tbsp dried mixed herbs such as
    oregano, thyme, sage, tarragon and dill
25 g/1 oz/¼ cup finely chopped
    pistachio nuts (optional)
350 g/12 oz puff pastry
60–90 ml/4–6 tbsp grated
    Parmesan cheese
1 egg, lightly beaten, for glazing
poppy seeds, sesame seeds, fennel seeds
    and aniseeds, for sprinkling
salt and freshly ground black pepper

1 In a small frying pan, over medium heat, melt the butter. Add the onion and cook for about 5 minutes until softened. Remove from the heat and cool. Put the onion, sausage meat, herbs, salt and pepper and nuts (if using) in a mixing bowl and stir together until blended.

2 Divide the sausage meat into four equal portions and roll into sausages about 25 cm/10 in long. Set aside. Preheat the oven to 220°C/425°F/ Gas 7. Lightly grease a baking sheet.

3 On a lightly floured surface, roll out the pastry to about 3 mm/⅛ in thick. Cut it into four strips measuring 25 x 7.5 cm/10 x 3 in. Place a long sausage on each pastry strip and sprinkle with a little Parmesan cheese.

4 Brush one long edge of each of the pastry strips with the egg glaze and roll up to enclose each sausage. Set them seam-side down and press gently to seal. Brush with the egg glaze and sprinkle with one type of seeds. Repeat with the remaining pastry strips and different seeds.

VARIATION: Filo pastry can be used instead of puff pastry for a very light effect.

5 Cut each of the pastry logs into
2.5 cm/1 in lengths and arrange on
the prepared baking sheet. Bake for
15 minutes until the pastry is crisp and
brown. Serve the sausage rolls warm or
at room temperature.

Skinny Dips

Children will adore scooping up the lightly spiced coriander dip with these scrumptiously crispy potato skins.

Serves 4

INGREDIENTS
8 large potatoes, scrubbed
30–45 ml/2–3 tbsp oil
90 ml/6 tbsp mayonnaise
30 ml/2 tbsp plain yogurt
5 ml/1 tsp curry paste
30 ml/2 tbsp roughly chopped fresh
    coriander, plus extra to garnish
salt

1 Preheat the oven to 190°C/375°F/ Gas 5. Arrange the potatoes in a roasting tin, prick them all over with a fork and cook for 45 minutes–1 hour or until tender. Leave to cool slightly.

2 Carefully cut each potato into quarters lengthways. Scoop out some of the centre with a knife or spoon and put the skins back in the roasting tin. (Save the cooked potato for use in other recipes.)

3 Brush the skins with oil and sprinkle with salt before returning them to the oven.

4 Cook the potato skins for 30–40 minutes more until they are crisp and brown, brushing them occasionally with more oil which will help to make the skins crisp.

5 Meanwhile, put the mayonnaise, plain yogurt, curry paste and 15 ml/ 1 tbsp of the chopped coriander in a small bowl and mix them together thoroughly. Leave the dip for 30–40 minutes to allow the flavour to develop fully.

6 Transfer the coriander dip to a serving bowl and place on a large platter. Arrange the hot potato skins around the bowl. Serve, sprinkled with the remaining coriander.

Tortilla Squares

Colourful little bites of baked omelette make appealing kids' party food.

Makes about 60 squares

INGREDIENTS
90 ml/6 tbsp olive oil, plus extra for brushing
1 large onion, thinly sliced
350 g/12 oz baking potatoes, thinly sliced
2 garlic cloves, finely chopped
2.5 ml/½ tsp dried thyme
8 eggs
5–10 ml/1–2 tsp dried oregano or basil
pinch of cayenne pepper (optional)
165 g/5½ oz/1¼ cups frozen peas, thawed
   and drained
45–60 ml/3–4 tbsp grated Parmesan cheese
salt and freshly ground black pepper
red pepper triangles, to garnish

1 In a large, deep, non-stick frying pan, heat 60 ml/4 tbsp of the oil over a medium heat. Add the onion and potatoes and cook for 8–10 minutes, stirring frequently, until just tender.

2 Add the garlic, thyme and seasoning and cook for 2 minutes longer. Remove from the heat and cool slightly.

3 Preheat the oven to 150°C/300°F/ Gas 2. Brush a 20 x 30 cm/8 x 12 in square baking dish with the remaining oil. In a bowl, beat the eggs with the oregano or basil, salt and cayenne, if using. Stir in the peas.

4 Spread the cooled potato mixture evenly into the baking dish and pour over the egg mixture. Bake for about 40 minutes until just set. Sprinkle with the cheese and bake for another 5 minutes. Remove to a wire rack.

5 When cool, cut the tortilla into 60 small squares. Serve warm or at room temperature with cocktail sticks and triangles of red pepper.

Glazed Spare Ribs

Temptingly coated with a sweet, sticky glaze, these are finger-licking good.

Makes about 25

INGREDIENTS
1 kg/2¼ lb meaty pork spare ribs,
    cut into 5 cm/2 in lengths
175 ml/6 fl oz/¾ cup tomato ketchup or
    mild chilli sauce
30–45 ml/2–3 tbsp soy sauce
30–45 ml/2–3 tbsp clear honey
2 garlic cloves, finely chopped
50 ml/2 fl oz/¼ cup orange juice
1.5 ml/¼ tsp cayenne pepper (optional)
1.5 ml/¼ tsp Chinese five-spice powder
1–2 star anise
lemon slices and shredded lettuce, to garnish

1 Using a small, sharp knife, scrape
away about 5 mm/¼ in of meat from
one end of each tiny spare rib to serve
as a little "handle".

2 In a large bowl or shallow baking
dish, mix together the ketchup or
chilli sauce, soy sauce, honey, garlic,
orange juice, cayenne pepper, if using,
Chinese five-spice powder and star
anise until well blended. Add the ribs
and toss to coat. Cover and chill for
6–8 hours or overnight.

3 Preheat the oven to 180°C/350°F/
Gas 4. Line a baking sheet with foil and
arrange the spare ribs in a single layer,
spooning over any remaining marinade.

4 Bake, uncovered, basting
occasionally, for 1–1½ hours or until
the ribs are well browned and glazed.
Serve warm or at room temperature,
garnished with lemon slices and
shredded lettuce.

Roly Poly Hedgehogs

A way of serving simple savoury food that children will find amusing. It is worth taking trouble over the hedgehog's face, which brings it to life.

Makes 4

INGREDIENTS
4 large baking potatoes
6–8 frankfurter sausages
50 g/2 oz cherry tomatoes
50 g/2 oz mild Cheddar cheese
2 celery sticks
small pieces of red pepper and black olive
1 carrot, chopped
shredded iceberg lettuce

3 Cut the tomatoes in half. When the sausages are cool enough to handle, cut them into 2.5 cm/1 in lengths. Cut the cheese into cubes and slice the celery. Spear the food on cocktail sticks in different combinations.

1 Preheat the oven to 200°C/400°F/ Gas 6. Prick the potatoes all over with a fork. Bake for 1–1¼ hours until soft (test with a skewer).

2 Meanwhile, heat the frankfurters in a large pan of boiling water for 8–10 minutes until warmed through. Drain and leave to cool slightly.

COOK'S TIP: You may prefer not to use cocktail sticks for serving food to very young children.

4 When the potatoes are cooked, remove them from the oven. Pierce the skin all over with the topped cocktail sticks.

5 Decorate each hedgehog's head with eyes made from red pepper and olive, and a carrot snout. Serve on a bed of shredded lettuce.

Margherita Pizza

Pizza is popular, particularly at parties, and it is so easy for small fingers to guide into little mouths!

Makes a 25–30 cm/
10–12 in pizza

INGREDIENTS
30 ml/2 tbsp olive oil
150 g/5 oz mozzarella cheese,
    thinly sliced
2 ripe tomatoes, thinly sliced
6–8 fresh basil leaves, roughly torn
30 ml/2 tbsp grated Parmesan cheese
freshly ground black pepper

FOR THE DOUGH
175 g/6 oz/1½ cups strong white flour, plus
    extra for dusting
1.5 ml/¼ tsp salt
5 ml/1 tsp easy-blend dried yeast
120–150 ml/4–5 fl oz/½–⅔ cup
    lukewarm water
15 ml/1 tbsp olive oil

FOR THE TOMATO SAUCE
1 onion, finely chopped
1 garlic clove, crushed
15 ml/1 tbsp olive oil
400 g/14 oz can chopped tomatoes
15 ml/1 tbsp tomato purée
15 ml/1 tbsp chopped fresh mixed herbs,
    such as oregano, basil and thyme
pinch of sugar

1 To make the dough, mix the flour, salt and yeast in a bowl. Make a well in the centre, add the water and oil and mix to a soft dough using a spoon.

2 Knead on a lightly floured surface for about 10 minutes until smooth and elastic. Place in a greased bowl, cover and leave in a warm place for about 1 hour or until doubled in size.

3 Meanwhile, to make the tomato sauce, fry the onion and garlic in the oil for 5 minutes. Add the remaining ingredients and seasoning. Simmer, stirring occasionally, for 15–20 minutes or until thick. Leave to cool.

4 Preheat the oven to 220°C/425°F/ Gas 7. Knock back the dough. Knead again for 2–3 minutes, then roll out to a 25–30 cm/10–12 in round and place on a greased baking sheet.

5 Brush the dough with 15 ml/1 tbsp of the oil and then spread over the tomato sauce. Arrange the mozzarella and sliced tomatoes on top.

6 Sprinkle with basil and Parmesan. Drizzle over the remaining oil and season with black pepper. Bake for 15–20 minutes until crisp and golden. Serve immediately, cut into wedges.

COOK'S TIP: Use a ready-made pizza base and sauce to save time.

Pizza Faces

These funny faces are easy to make and are a great hit with kids.

Makes 9

INGREDIENTS
30 ml/2 tbsp vegetable oil
1 onion, finely shredded
200 g/7 oz can chopped tomatoes
25 g/1 oz tomato purée
9 crumpets
200 g/7 oz processed cheese slices
1 green pepper, seeded and chopped into
    small pieces
4–5 cherry tomatoes, sliced
salt and freshly ground
    black pepper

1 Preheat the oven to 220°C/425°F/ Gas 7. Heat the oil in a large pan, add the onion and cook for 2–3 minutes until softened.

2 Add the canned tomatoes, tomato purée and seasoning. Bring to the boil and cook for 5–6 minutes until the mixture becomes thick and pulpy. Leave to cool.

3 Lightly toast the crumpets under the grill. Lay them on a baking sheet. Put a heaped teaspoon of the tomato mixture on the top and spread it out evenly. Bake in the oven for 25 minutes.

4 Cut the cheese slices into strips and arrange them with the green pepper and cherry tomatoes on top of the pizzas to make smiling faces. Return to the oven for about 5 minutes until the cheese melts. Serve the pizzas while still warm.

Nutty Chicken Kebabs

A tasty party dish that uses everyone's favourite spread in the dip.

Serves 4

INGREDIENTS
30 ml/2 tbsp oil
15 ml/1 tbsp lemon juice
450 g/1 lb skinless boneless chicken breasts,
    cut into small cubes

FOR THE DIP
5 ml/1 tsp chilli powder
75 ml/5 tbsp water
15 ml/1 tbsp oil
1 small onion, grated
1 garlic clove, crushed
30 ml/2 tbsp lemon juice
60 ml/4 tbsp crunchy peanut butter
5 ml/1 tsp salt
5 ml/1 tsp ground coriander
cucumber slices and lemon wedges, to serve

1 Soak 12 wooden skewers in water, to prevent them from burning during grilling. Mix the oil and lemon juice in a bowl and stir in the chicken. Cover and marinate for at least 30 minutes.

2 Thread four or five cubes on each skewer. Cook under a hot grill, turning often, for about 10 minutes until cooked and browned.

3 Meanwhile, mix the chilli powder with 15 ml/1 tbsp water. Heat the oil in a frying pan and fry the onion and garlic until tender, then turn down the heat and stir in the remaining ingredients. Add more water if needed. Serve warm, with the kebabs, cucumber slices and lemon wedges.

Chicken Lollipops

These tasty stuffed wings, which children can hold and eat like sweet lollipops, will go down very well.

Makes 12

INGREDIENTS
12 large chicken wings
oil, for deep-frying

FOR THE FILLING
5 ml/1 tsp cornflour
1.5 ml/¼ tsp salt
2.5 ml/½ tsp fresh thyme
pinch of freshly ground
   black pepper

FOR THE COATING
225 g/8 oz/3 cups dried breadcrumbs
30 ml/2 tbsp sesame seeds
2 eggs, beaten

2 Holding the large end of the bone on the third section of the wing and using a sharp knife, cut the skin and flesh away from the bone, scraping down and pulling the meat over the small end, forming a pocket. Repeat this process with all the remaining wing sections.

3 Fill the tiny pockets with the filling. To make the coating for the lollipops, mix the breadcrumbs and the sesame seeds together. Place the breadcrumb mixture and the beaten egg in separate dishes.

4 Brush the chicken lollipops with beaten egg and roll in breadcrumbs to cover. Chill and repeat to give a second layer, forming a thick coating. Chill until ready to fry.

5 Preheat the oven to 180°C/350°F/ Gas 4. Heat 5 cm/2 in of oil in a heavy-based pan until hot but not smoking or the breadcrumbs will burn.

1 Remove the wing tips and discard or use them for making stock. Skin the second joint sections, removing the two small bones; take the meat off these bones, mince and mix with the filling ingredients in a bowl.

6 Gently fry two or three lollipops at a time until golden brown. Remove and drain on kitchen paper. Complete the cooking in the preheated oven for 15–20 minutes or until tender. Serve warm or at room temperature.

Aduki Bean Burgers

Really delicious burgers, served with all the trimmings, that will please young vegetarian party guests who are fussy about their food.

Makes 12

INGREDIENTS
200 g/7 oz/1 cup brown rice
1 onion, chopped
2 garlic cloves, crushed
30 ml/2 tbsp sunflower oil
50 g/2 oz/¼ cup butter
1 small green pepper, seeded and chopped
1 carrot, coarsely grated
400 g/14 oz can aduki beans, drained and
    rinsed, or 115 g/4 oz/¾ cup dried weight,
    soaked and cooked
1 egg, beaten
115 g/4 oz/1 cup mature cheese, grated
5 ml/1 tsp dried thyme
50 g/2 oz/½ cup roasted hazelnuts or toasted
    flaked almonds
wholemeal flour or cornmeal, for coating
oil, for deep-frying
salt and freshly ground black pepper
burger buns, salad and relishes, to serve

1 Cook the rice according to the instructions on the packet, allowing it to overcook slightly so that it is soft. Drain and transfer to a large bowl.

COOK'S TIP: These burgers freeze very successfully. Cool them after cooking, open-freeze, wrap and bag. Use within 6 weeks. Bake from frozen in a preheated oven at 180°C/ 350°F/Gas 4 for 20–25 minutes.

2 Fry the onion and garlic in the oil and butter together with the chopped green pepper and grated carrot for about 10 minutes until the vegetables are softened.

3 Stir the cooked vegetables into the rice with the aduki beans, egg, cheese, thyme, nuts and plenty of seasoning. Chill until quite firm.

4 Shape into 12 patties, wetting your hands if the mixture sticks. Coat the patties in wholemeal flour or cornmeal and set aside.

5 Heat 1 cm/½ in oil in a large, shallow frying pan and fry the burgers in batches for about 5 minutes until brown, turning after 3 minutes. Remove and drain on kitchen paper. Serve hot in burger buns with salad and relishes.

Ice Cream Bombes

This chilly dessert with warm sauce is simply dynamite for kids!

Serves 6

INGREDIENTS
1 litre/1¾ pints/4 cups soft-scoop
    chocolate ice cream
475 ml/16 fl oz/2 cups soft-scoop
    vanilla ice cream
50 g/2 oz/⅓ cup plain
    chocolate drops
115 g/4 oz toffees
75 ml/5 tbsp double cream

1 Divide the soft-scoop chocolate ice cream among six small cups. Push it roughly to the base and up the sides, leaving a small, cup-shaped hollow in the middle. Do not worry if the ice cream is not arranged very neatly; it will be frozen again before the ice cream melts too much.

2 Return to the freezer and leave for 45 minutes. Take out again and smooth into shape. Return to the freezer.

3 Put the vanilla ice cream in a small bowl and break it up slightly. Stir in the chocolate drops and use to fill the hollow in the chocolate ice cream. Return to the freezer overnight.

4 Put the toffees in a small saucepan and heat gently, stirring all the time. As they melt, add the double cream and keep mixing until all the toffees have melted and the sauce is warm.

5 Dip the cups in hot water and run a knife round the edge of the ice cream. Turn out on to plates, pour the sauce over and serve.

Puffy Pears

An eye-catching dessert that looks great on a kids' party table.

Serves 4

INGREDIENTS
225 g/8 oz ready-made puff pastry
2 pears, peeled, halved and cored
2 squares plain chocolate, roughly chopped
15 ml/1 tbsp lemon juice
1 egg, beaten
15 ml/1 tbsp caster sugar
icing sugar, for dusting (optional)

1 Roll out the puff pastry into a 25 cm/10 in square on a lightly floured surface. Trim the edges, then cut it into four equal smaller squares.

2 Pack the hollow in each pear half with the chopped chocolate. Place a pear half, cut-side down, on each piece of pastry and brush with lemon juice.

3 Preheat the oven to 190°C/375°F/Gas 5. Cut the puff pastry into a pear shape, by following the lines of the fruit, leaving a 2.5 cm/1 in border all around.

4 Use the trimmings to make leaves and brush the pastry border with the beaten egg.

5 Arrange the pastry and pears on a baking sheet. Make deep cuts in the pears, taking care not to cut right through the fruit, and sprinkle them with the caster sugar.

6 Bake the pears for 20–25 minutes until they are lightly browned. Serve hot or cold, dusted with icing sugar if you wish.

Monster Meringues

Children will be clamouring for more of these crisp, mouth-watering meringues, whipped cream and tangy summer fruits.

Serves 4

INGREDIENTS
3 egg whites
175 g/6 oz/¾ cup caster sugar
15 ml/1 tbsp cornflour
5 ml/1 tsp white wine vinegar
few drops of vanilla essence
225 g/8 oz/1½ cups assorted red
    summer fruits
300 ml/½ pint/1¼ cups
    double cream
1 passion fruit

1 Preheat the oven to 140°C/275°F/Gas 1. Using a pencil, draw eight 10 cm/4 in circles on two sheets of non-stick baking paper which will fit on two baking sheets. Place the paper face-down on the baking sheets.

2 Whisk the egg whites until they are stiff, then gradually add the caster sugar, whisking well after each separate addition until the mixture has become very stiff.

3 Using a metal spoon, gently stir in the cornflour, vinegar and vanilla essence. Put the meringue mixture into a large piping bag fitted with a large star nozzle.

4 Pipe a solid layer of meringue in four of the drawn circles and then pipe a lattice pattern in the other four. Cook in the oven for 1¼–1½ hours, swapping the shelf positions after 30 minutes, until lightly browned. The paper will peel off the back easily when the meringues are cooked. Allow to cool.

5 Roughly chop most of the summer fruits, reserving a few for decoration. Whip the cream and spread it over the solid meringue shapes. Scatter the chopped fruit on top. Halve the passion fruit, scoop out the seeds with a teaspoon and scatter them over. Top with a lattice lid and serve with the reserved whole fruits.

Kooky Cookies

Cut out these easy cookies in lots of different shapes and let your imagination run wild with the decorating, using lots of bright colours.

Makes 20

INGREDIENTS
115 g/4 oz/1 cup self-raising flour
5 ml/1 tsp ground ginger
5 ml/1 tsp bicarbonate of soda
50 g/2 oz/¼ cup sugar
50 g/2 oz/¼ cup butter, softened
30 ml/2 tbsp golden syrup

FOR THE ICING
115 g/4 oz/½ cup butter, softened
225 g/8 oz/2 cups sifted
    icing sugar
5 ml/1 tsp lemon juice
few drops of food colouring
coloured writing icing
coloured sweets

1 Sift the self-raising flour, ground ginger and bicarbonate of soda into a large mixing bowl. Add the sugar, then carefully rub in the softened butter with your fingertips, lifting the mixture above the bowl, until it resembles fine breadcrumbs.

2 Add the golden syrup and mix to a dough. Preheat the oven to 190°C/375°F/Gas 5. Grease a baking sheet.

3 Roll out to 3 mm/⅛ in thick on a lightly floured surface. Stamp out shapes with biscuit cutters and transfer to the prepared baking sheet. Bake for 5–10 minutes before transferring to a wire rack to cool.

4 To make the icing, beat the butter in a bowl until light and fluffy. Add the icing sugar a little at a time and continue beating. Add the lemon juice and food colouring. Spread over some of the cooled cookies and leave to set.

5 To make each cookie individual, decorate some with coloured sweets just before the icing has set completely. Leave the other cookies until the icing has set and then decorate them with a variety of coloured writing icing.

Mint-surprise Chocolate Cupcakes

Exclamations of delight will be heard as children discover the creamy, mint filling that is hidden within these little cupcakes, which are also topped with minty chocolate icing.

Makes 12

INGREDIENTS
225 g/8 oz/2 cups plain flour
5 ml/1 tsp bicarbonate of soda
pinch of salt
50 g/2 oz/½ cup unsweetened
   cocoa powder
150 g/5 oz/10 tbsp unsalted
   butter, softened
300 g/11 oz/1½ cups
   caster sugar
3 eggs
5 ml/1 tsp peppermint essence
250 ml/8 fl oz/1 cup milk

FOR THE MINT CREAM FILLING
300 ml/½ pint/1¼ cups double or
   whipping cream
5 ml/1 tsp peppermint essence

FOR THE CHOCOLATE MINT GLAZE
175 g/6 oz plain chocolate
115 g/4 oz/½ cup unsalted butter
5 ml/1 tsp peppermint essence

1 Preheat the oven to 180°C/350°F/ Gas 4. Line a 12-hole bun tray with individual paper cases. Into a mixing bowl, sift together the flour, bicarbonate of soda, pinch of salt and cocoa powder.

2 Using a hand-held electric mixer, beat the butter and sugar in a large mixing bowl until light and creamy.

3 Add the eggs to the butter and sugar one at a time, beating well after each addition, then beat in the peppermint essence. On low speed, beat in the flour mixture alternately with the milk until just blended. Spoon into the prepared paper cases.

4 Bake for 12–15 minutes until a thin skewer inserted in the centre of a bun comes out clean: do not over-bake.

5 Immediately remove the cupcakes from the tin to a wire rack to cool completely. When they are cool, remove the paper cases.

6 To make the filling, whip the cream and peppermint essence in a small bowl until stiff peaks form. Spoon into a small icing bag fitted with a small, plain tip. Push the tip into the bottom of a cupcake and squeeze gently, releasing about 15 ml/1 tbsp of cream into the centre. Repeat with the remaining cupcakes.

7 To make the glaze, melt the chocolate and butter in a saucepan over low heat, stirring until smooth. Remove from the heat and stir in the peppermint essence. Cool, then spread on top of each cake.

Chunky Choc Bars

An easy cake that needs no cooking and is a smash-hit with kids.

Makes 12

INGREDIENTS
350 g/12 oz plain chocolate
115 g/4 oz/½ cup butter
400 g/14 oz can condensed milk
225 g/8 oz digestive biscuits, broken
50 g/2 oz/⅓ cup raisins
115 g/4 oz/⅔ cup ready-to-eat dried peaches,
   roughly chopped
50 g/2 oz/½ cup hazelnuts or pecans,
   roughly chopped

2 Beat the condensed milk into the chocolate and butter mixture. Add the biscuits, raisins, peaches and nuts and mix well until all the ingredients are coated in chocolate.

3 Tip the mixture into the prepared tin, making sure it is pressed well into the corners. Leave the top craggy. Put in the fridge and leave to set.

1 Line an 18 x 28 cm/7 x 11 in cake tin with clear film. Put the chocolate and butter in a large bowl over a pan of hot but not boiling water (the bowl must not touch the water) and leave to melt. Stir until well mixed.

4 Lift the cake out of the tin using the clear film and then carefully peel it off. Cut the cake into 12 bars and keep chilled until ready to serve.

VARIATION: Experiment with different fruits and nuts. Try replacing the peaches with chopped dried apples and the chopped hazelnuts or pecans with toasted blanched almonds.

Basic Cake

All the designs that follow are based on this basic cake recipe. For larger cakes, simply increase the quantities as indicated in the individual recipes and follow the steps below.

Makes a 15 cm/6 in round or square cake

INGREDIENTS
2 eggs
115 g/4 oz/½ cup caster sugar
115 g/4 oz/½ cup butter or margarine
115 g/4 oz/1 cup self-raising flour
2.5 ml/½ tsp baking powder
15 ml/1 tbsp water

1 Preheat the oven to 190°C/375°F/ Gas 5. Lightly grease the base and sides of a 15 cm/6 in round cake tin with melted butter or margarine. Base-line with greaseproof paper, then grease the paper.

2 Put the eggs, sugar, butter or margarine and flour into a bowl. Measure the baking powder level with a knife and then add to the other ingredients in the bowl. Add the water. Whisk all the cake ingredients together until smooth and creamy.

3 Spoon the cake mixture into the prepared tin and spread evenly to the sides.

4 Bake in the centre of the oven for 35–45 minutes or until a thin skewer inserted into the centre of the cake comes out clean. Loosen the sides of the cake carefully with a knife.

5 Cover a wire cooling rack with a piece of greaseproof paper (this will prevent the cake from sticking) and carefully turn the cake on to the wire rack. Allow the cake to cool completely before icing.

Royal Icing

This is used for piping, run-outs and sticking decorations on to cakes. It dries very hard and holds its shape when piped.

Makes 225 g/8 oz/2 cups

INGREDIENTS
1 large egg white
225 g/8 oz/2 cups icing sugar, sifted

1 Whisk the egg white in a large bowl with a fork. Add a quarter of the icing sugar and beat well.

2 Gradually work in the remaining icing sugar, beating well between each addition, until the icing mixture holds its shape.

3 Lay a piece of clear film on top of the icing and cover the bowl with a damp cloth to prevent the icing drying out. Store at room temperature.

COOK'S TIP: Dried egg white powder, which is available from supermarkets, may be used. It is whisked together with water and sifted icing sugar, following the instructions on the packet. Icing made this way must also be covered at all times, as it dries very quickly.

Butter Icing

This is used as a filling, to sandwich cakes together.

Makes 65 g/2½ oz/⅔ cup

INGREDIENTS
15 g/½ oz/1 tbsp butter
7.5 ml/1½ tsp milk
50 g/2 oz/½ cup icing sugar, sifted

Soften the butter, gradually add the milk and whisk in the sifted icing sugar until smooth and glossy. Add any flavouring and colouring required by the recipe.

Quick Fondant Icing

This is soft and pliable and must be worked with fairly quickly, as it will dry out. It should be wrapped securely in clear film if you are not using it. Roll out on a smooth surface dusted with a little sifted icing sugar or cornflour. It stays fairly soft for cutting and eating.

Makes 500 g/1¼ lb/5 cups

INGREDIENTS

500 g/1¼ lb/5 cups icing sugar, sifted
1 large egg white
30 ml/2 tbsp liquid glucose
cornflour

1 Put the icing sugar, egg white and glucose into a food processor and blend together until the mixture resembles fine breadcrumbs.

2 Knead the mixture with your hands until it becomes smooth and pliable, like dough. A drop of water may be added if the mixture is too dry. A little cornflour may be added to prevent it becoming sticky. It is ready when it no longer feels sticky and can be rolled out. (The whole process can be done by hand in a bowl.)

Marzipan

All the cakes are covered with a layer of marzipan. It seals in the moisture and gives a smooth, flat surface on which to ice. It is easy to work with and useful for modelling. If your children do not like marzipan, replace it with a layer of fondant.

Makes 675 g/1½ lb/5 cups

INGREDIENTS

225 g/8 oz/2 cups ground almonds
275 g/10 oz/1½ cups caster sugar
175 g/6 oz/1½ cups icing sugar
1 egg
15–30 ml/1–2 tbsp
    lemon juice
2.5 ml/½ tsp almond essence

1 Mix all the dry ingredients in a bowl. Add the egg, the lemon juice and almond essence to the ground almond mixture.

2 Mix thoroughly to form a pliable paste. Wrap in clear film until needed. Roll out on a surface lightly dusted with a little sifted icing sugar.

Apricot Glaze

This is used to seal the cake and stop the crumbs working their way into the icing. It will also stick the marzipan or fondant to the cake.

Makes 175 g/6 oz/½ cup

INGREDIENTS

175 g/6 oz/½ cup apricot jam
15 ml/1 tbsp water

Heat the apricot jam in a pan with the water, then rub through a sieve to remove any lumps. Return to the pan and heat until boiling before brushing carefully over the cake.

COOK'S TIP: The layer of apricot glaze will also prevent the icing from turning dull and dry, as the moisture in the icing will remain there, rather than being drawn out and absorbed by the cake.

Lining a Cake Tin

Lining tins is important so that the cakes can be turned out without breaking or sticking to the base. This method is simple, but essential.

1 Place the tin on a piece of greaseproof paper, draw around the base with a pencil and cut out the paper inside this line.

2 Grease the base and sides of the tin with melted butter or soft margarine and stick the piece of paper in neatly. Grease the paper on top. The tin is now ready for filling.

COOK'S TIP: If you make a lot of cakes, it is worth making several linings at once and storing them flat in a polythene bag.

Drum

This is a colourful cake for very young children, who will find it so realistic that they may want to play it!

Makes a 15 cm/6 in round cake

INGREDIENTS
15 cm/6 in round cake
50 g/2 oz/¼ cup butter icing
apricot glaze
350 g/12 oz/2¼ cups marzipan
450 g/1 lb/4 cups quick
    fondant icing
red, blue and yellow
    food colourings

1 Split the cake and fill with the butter icing. Place on a 20 cm/8 in round cake board and brush with the hot apricot glaze. Cover the cake with a layer of marzipan and leave it to dry overnight.

2 Colour half the fondant icing red. Reserve a small amount for the drumsticks, then roll out to 25 x 30 cm/10 x 12 in and cut in half. Stick to the sides of the cake with water, smoothing the joins neatly.

3 Reserve a little white icing for the drumsticks, then roll out a circle to fit the top of the cake.

4 Divide the rest of the fondant icing in half. Colour one half blue and the other yellow. Divide the blue into four equal pieces and roll each piece into a sausage long enough to go half way round the cake. Stick around the base and top of the cake with a little water.

5 Using a sharp knife, mark the blue edging of the cake into six around the top and bottom using a circle of greaseproof paper that has been folded to show six wedges.

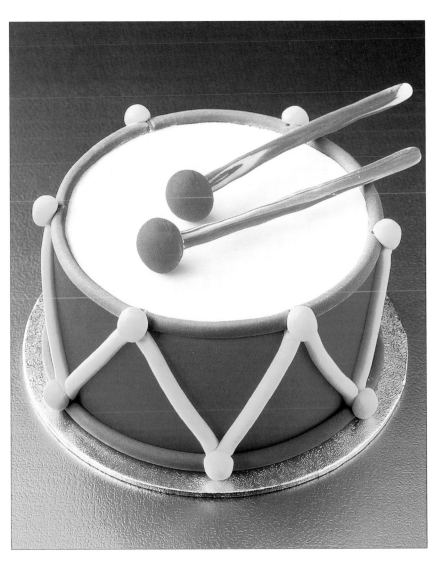

6 Roll the yellow fondant icing into strands long enough to cross diagonally from top to bottom to form the drum strings. Roll the rest of the yellow fondant icing into 12 small balls and stick where the strings join the drum.

7 Using the remaining red and white fondant icing, knead together until streaky and roll two balls and sticks 15 cm/6 in long. Dry overnight. Stick together with a little royal icing to make the drumsticks.

Teddy's Birthday

Young children will adore this jolly-faced teddy bear with his own cake.

Makes a 20 cm/8 in round cake

INGREDIENTS
20 cm/8 in round cake
115 g/4 oz/1¼ cups butter icing
apricot glaze
350 g/12 oz/2½ cups marzipan
450 g/1 lb/4 cups quick fondant icing
brown, pink, red, blue and black
    food colourings
115 g/4 oz/¾ cup royal icing
silver balls
1.5 m/1½ yds ribbon, 2.5 cm/1 in wide, and
    candles, to decorate

1 Split the cake and fill with the butter icing. Place on a 25 cm/10 in round cake board and brush with hot apricot glaze. Cover with a layer of marzipan, then fondant icing. Using a template, mark the design on top of the cake.

2 Colour one-third of the remaining fondant icing pale brown. Colour a piece pink, a piece red, some blue and a tiny piece black. Using a template, cut out the pieces to make the teddy.

3 Place the pieces in position. Stick down by lifting the edges and brushing the undersides with water. Roll ovals for the eyes and stick in place with the nose and eyebrows. Cut out a mouth and press flat.

4 Tie the ribbon around the cake. Colour the royal icing blue and pipe a border around the base of the cake using a no. 7 shell tube.

5 Pipe tiny stars around the small cake using a no. 7 star tube and inserting silver balls. Place the candles on the small cake.

COOK'S TIP: For a 20 cm/8 in round cake, follow the instructions for the 15 cm/6 in cake, but use three eggs, 175 g/6 oz/¾ cup caster sugar, 175 g/6 oz/¾ cup butter or margarine, 175 g/6 oz/1½ cups self-raising flour, 4 ml/¾ tsp baking powder and 30 ml/2 tbsp water. Bake for 45–55 minutes.

Ballerina

This cake requires patience and plenty of time for the decoration.

Makes a 20 cm/8 in round cake

INGREDIENTS
20 cm/8 in round cake
115 g/4 oz/1¼ cups butter icing
apricot glaze
450 g/1 lb/3 cups marzipan
450 g/1 lb/4 cups quick fondant icing
pink, green, yellow, brown and blue
    food colourings
115 g/4 oz/¾ cup royal icing
1.5 m/1½ yds ribbon, 2.5 cm/1 in wide

1 Split the cake and fill with the butter icing. Place on a 25 cm/10 in round cake board and brush with hot apricot glaze. Cover with a layer of marzipan then a layer of fondant icing. Leave to dry overnight.

2 Divide the remaining fondant icing into three; colour one flesh tones and the other two contrasting pinks. Roll out each colour and use 5 mm/¼ in and 9 mm/ ⅜ in flower cutters with ejectors to cut out 12 flowers and three tiny flowers from the paler pink fondant. Set aside to dry.

3 Using a template, carefully mark the position of the ballerina. Cut out the body from flesh-coloured icing and stick in position with water. Round off the edges gently with a finger. Cut out a bodice from the darker pink fondant and stick in place.

4 To make the tutu, work swiftly as the thin fondant dries quickly and will crack. Roll out the darker pink fondant to 3 mm/⅛ in thick and cut out a fluted circle with a small plain inner circle. Cut into quarters and, with a cocktail stick, roll along the fluted edge to stretch it and give it fullness.

5 Attach the frills to the waist with a little water. Repeat with two more layers, using a cocktail stick to shape the frills and cotton wool to hold them in place until dry. For the final layer of frills, use the paler pink fondant and cover with a short dark frill, as the bodice extension. Leave to dry overnight.

6 Attach flowers as the hoop. Colour a little royal icing green and pipe tiny leaves. Paint on the face and hair. Stick tiny flowers around the head. Cut pale pink shoes and stick on, and paint ribbons. Pipe the flower centres from dark pink royal icing. Pipe royal icing around the base with a no. 7 shell tube. Tie with pink ribbon, to decorate.

COOK'S TIP: For this size cake, follow the steps for the 15 cm/6 in cake, but use three eggs, 175 g/6 oz/ ¾ cup sugar, 175 g/6 oz/¾ cup butter or margarine, 175 g/6 oz/ 1½ cups flour, 4 ml/¾ tsp baking powder and 30 ml/2 tbsp water. Bake for 45–55 minutes.

Racing Track

A cake to thrill all eight-year old racing-car enthusiasts. It is relatively simple to make and can be decorated with as many cars as you like.

Makes 1 cake

INGREDIENTS
2 (15 cm/6 in) round cakes
115 g/4 oz/1¼ cups butter icing
500 g/1¼ lb/5 cups quick
    fondant icing
blue and red food colourings
apricot glaze
450 g/1 lb/3 cups marzipan
115 g/4 oz/¾ cup royal icing
candles and 2 small racing cars,
    to decorate

1 Split the cakes and fill with the butter icing. Cut off a 1 cm/½ in piece from one side of each cake and then place both the cakes on a 25 x 35 cm/ 10 x 14 in cake board with the flat edges together.

2 Colour about 450 g/1 lb/4½ cups of the fondant icing pale blue. Brush the cakes with hot apricot glaze. Cover with a layer of marzipan, then with the pale blue fondant icing.

3 Mark a 5 cm/2 in circle in the centre of each cake. Roll out the remaining white fondant icing, cut out two fluted circles and stick in the marked spaces.

4 Colour the royal icing red. Pipe a shell border around the base of the cake using a no. 8 star tube.

5 Pipe a track for the cars on the cake using a no. 2 plain tube. Place the candles on the two white circles and arrange the cars on the track.

Computer Game

The perfect cake to bake for a computer game fanatic.

Makes 1 cake

INGREDIENTS
15 cm/6 in square cake
115 g/4 oz/1¼ cups butter icing
apricot glaze
275 g/10 oz/1¾ cups quick
    fondant icing
black, blue, red and yellow
    food colourings
225 g/8 oz/1½ cups marzipan
royal icing

1 Split the cake and fill with the butter icing. With a sharp, serrated knife, cut 2.5 cm/1 in off one side of the cake and 1 cm/½ in off the other. Round the corners slightly. Place on a 20 cm/8 in square cake board and brush with hot apricot glaze.

2 Colour 225 g/8 oz/1½ cups of the fondant icing black. Cover the cake with a layer of marzipan, then with most of the black fondant icing.

3 With a wooden cocktail stick, mark the speaker holes and position of the screen and knobs.

4 Colour half the remaining white fondant icing pale blue, roll out and cut out a 6 cm/2½ in square for the screen. Stick in the centre of the game with a little water.

5 Colour a small piece of fondant icing red and the rest yellow. Cut out the start switch 2.5 cm/1 in long from the red and the controls from the yellow. Stick into position with water.

6 Roll the remaining black fondant into a long, thin sausage and use it to edge the screen and around the base of the cake.

7 With a fine paintbrush, draw the game on to the screen with a little blue colour. Pipe letters on to the buttons with a little royal icing.

Smiley Kite

The face on this happy kite is a great favourite with children of all ages.

Makes 1 cake

INGREDIENTS
25 cm/10 in square cake
225 g/8 oz/2⅓ cups butter icing
apricot glaze
675 g/1½ lb/6⅔ cups quick fondant icing
yellow, red, green, blue and black
    food colourings
450 g/1 lb/3 cups marzipan
115 g/4 oz/¾ cup royal icing

1 Split the cake and fill with the butter icing. Mark 15 cm/6 in from one corner down two sides and, using a ruler from this point, cut down to the opposite corner on both sides to get the kite shape. Place diagonally on a 30 cm/12 in square cake board and brush with hot apricot glaze.

2 Colour 450 g/1 lb/3 cups of the fondant icing pale yellow. Divide the remainder into five portions leaving one white and colour the other four red, green, blue and black. Wrap each piece separately in clear film.

3 Cover the cake with a layer of marzipan, then a layer of the yellow fondant, leaving some for the tail.

4 Using a template, mark the happy face on the kite. Pipe a shell border around the base of the cake. Cut out the face, bow tie and buttons from the different colours of fondant icing and stick in place with a little water.

5 To make the kite's tail, roll out each colour separately and cut two 4 x 1 cm/ 1½ x ½ in lengths from the blue, red and green fondants. Pinch them to shape into bows.

COOK'S TIP: For a 25 cm/10 in square cake, follow the steps for the 15 cm/6 in round cake, but use eight eggs, 450 g/1 lb/2¼ cups caster sugar, 450 g/1 lb/2 cups butter or margarine, 450 g/1 lb/4 cups self-raising flour, 10 ml/2 tsp baking powder and 105 ml/7 tbsp water. Bake for 1½–1¾ hours.

6 Roll most of the remaining yellow into a long rope and lay it on the board in a wavy line from the narrow end of the kite, then stick the bows in place with water. Roll balls of yellow fondant, stick on the board with a little royal icing and press in candles.

Buck's Fizzy & Twizzles

A corker of a drink, which will knock spots off the real thing. Serve with savoury cheese twizzles.

Serves 6–8

INGREDIENTS
FOR THE BUCK'S FIZZY
600 ml/1 pint/2½ cups fresh orange juice
45 ml/3 tbsp lemon juice
50 g/2 oz/½ cup icing sugar, sifted
300 ml/½ pint/1¼ cups bitter
   lemon, chilled
orange slices, to decorate

FOR THE TWIZZLES
225 g/8 oz/2 cups plain flour
115 g/4 oz/½ cup butter, roughly chopped
15 ml/1 tbsp dried mixed herbs
50 g/2 oz/½ cup grated mature
   Cheddar cheese
cold water, to mix
salt and freshly ground black pepper

1 To make the Buck's fizzy, mix the orange and lemon juice and the icing sugar in a jug; stir and chill.

2 Just before serving, add the bitter lemon and decorate with orange slices.

3 To make the twizzles, preheat the oven to 190°C/375°F/Gas 5. Put the flour and the butter in a large bowl. Rub the butter into the flour with your fingertips until the mixture resembles breadcrumbs.

4 Stir in the herbs, cheese and seasoning and add enough water to make a firm dough. Knead into a ball.

5 Roll out the dough to a thickness of 5 mm/¼ in and cut it into 15 cm/6 in strips about 1 cm/½ in wide. Twist each strip once or twice and arrange them in rows on a greased baking sheet.

6 Bake for 15–20 minutes until golden brown. Cool the twizzles on a wire rack before serving with the Buck's fizzy.

COOK'S TIP: Make some of the pastry strips into circles. After baking, slip three pastry strips inside each circle so each guest gets his or her personal set of twizzles.

Strawberry Smoothie & Stars-in-your-eyes Biscuits

Kids are sure to find this creamy fruit drink, served with temptingly pretty little biscuits, very more-ish.

Serves 4–6

INGREDIENTS
FOR THE STRAWBERRY SMOOTHIE
225 g/8 oz/2 cups strawberries
150 ml/¼ pint/⅔ cup Greek yogurt
475 ml/16 fl oz/2 cups
   ice-cold milk
30 ml/2 tbsp icing sugar

FOR STARS-IN-YOUR-EYES BISCUITS
115 g/4 oz/½ cup butter
175 g/6 oz/1½ cups plain flour
50 g/2 oz/¼ cup caster sugar
30 ml/2 tbsp golden syrup
30 ml/2 tbsp preserving sugar

1 To make the stars-in-your-eyes biscuits, put the butter and flour in a bowl and rub in the fat with your fingertips until the mixture resembles breadcrumbs. Stir in the caster sugar and then knead together to make a ball. Chill for 30 minutes.

2 Preheat the oven to 180°C/350°F/ Gas 4 and lightly grease two baking sheets. Roll out the dough on a floured surface to a 5 mm/¼ in thickness and use a 7.5 cm/3 in star-shaped cutter to stamp out the biscuits.

3 Arrange the biscuits on the prepared baking sheet, leaving enough room for them to rise. Bake them for 10–15 minutes until golden brown.

4 Put the syrup in a small microwave-safe bowl and heat it on HIGH for 12 seconds or heat for 1–2 minutes over simmering water. Brush over the biscuits while they are still warm. Sprinkle a little preserving sugar on top of each one and leave to cool.

5 To make the smoothie, reserve a few strawberries for decoration and whizz the rest in a food processor or blender with the yogurt until smooth.

6 Add the milk and icing sugar, process the mixture again and pour into glasses. Serve each glass decorated with one or two of the reserved strawberries and accompanied by the stars-in-your-eyes biscuits.

Fruit Crush & Fruit Kebabs

Fruit crush, accompanied by mouth-watering fruit kebabs, is just the ticket for a children's party on a sultry summer's day.

Serves 6

INGREDIENTS

FOR THE FRUIT CRUSH
300 ml/½ pint/1¼ cups orange juice
300 ml/½ pint/1¼ cups
    pineapple juice
300 ml/½ pint/1¼ cups tropical
    fruit juice
475 ml/16 fl oz/2 cups lemonade
fresh pineapple slices and cherries,
    to decorate

FOR THE FRUIT KEBABS
24 small strawberries
24 seedless green grapes
12 marshmallows
1 kiwi fruit, peeled and cut in
    12 wedges
1 banana
15 ml/1 tbsp lemon juice

2 Mix together the tropical fruit juice and lemonade in a large jug. Put a mixture of the ice cubes in each glass and pour the fruit crush over. Decorate the glasses with the fresh pineapple slices and cherries.

3 To make the fruit kebabs, thread two small strawberries, two seedless green grapes, a marshmallow and a wedge of kiwi fruit on to each of 12 wooden skewers.

1 To make the fruit crush, put the orange juice and the pineapple juice into ice-cube trays and freeze them until solid.

4 Peel the banana and cut it into 12 slices. Toss it in the lemon juice and thread on to the skewers. Serve immediately with the fruit crush.

This edition is published by Southwater

Southwater is an imprint of
Anness Publishing Ltd
Hermes House
88–89 Blackfriars Road
London SE1 8HA
tel. 020 7401 2077
fax 020 7633 9499

Distributed in the USA by
Anness Publishing Inc.
27 West 20th Street
Suite 504, New York NY 10011

Distributed in the UK by
The Manning Partnership
251–253 London Road East
Batheaston
Bath BA1 7RL
tel. 01225 852 727
fax 01225 852 852

Distributed in Australia by
Sandstone Publishing
Unit 1, 360 Norton Street, Leichhardt
New South Wales 2040
tel. 02 9560 7888
fax 02 9560 7488

Publisher: Joanna Lorenz
Editor: Valerie Ferguson
Series Designer: Bobbie Colgate Stone
Designer: Andrew Heath
Production Controller: Joanna King

Recipes contributed by: Roz Denny, Shirley Gill, Carole Handslip, Bridget Jones, Sue Maggs, Judy Williams, Elizabeth Wolf-Cohen.

Photography: Karl Adamson, Edward Allwright, James Duncan, Amanda Heywood, David Jordan, Michael Michaels.

1 3 5 7 9 10 8 6 4 2

Notes:

For all recipes, quantities are given in both metric and imperial measures and, where appropriate, measures are also given in standard cups and spoons.
Follow one set, but not a mixture, because they are not interchangeable.

Standard spoon and cup measures are level.

1 tsp = 5 ml   1 tbsp = 15 ml

1 cup = 250 ml/8 fl oz

Australian standard tablespoons are 20 ml. Australian readers should use 3 tsp in place of 1 tbsp for measuring small quantities of gelatine, cornflour, salt etc.

Medium eggs are used unless otherwise stated.

64